# HOW TO TALK TO YOUR CUSTOMER

*A Simple guide to an effective communication between you and your Customer*

By

Gabriel Clinton

# Table of contents

# Introduction

# Chapter 1
**What Is Client Correspondence?**
What is Client Correspondence with
The executives (CCM)?
Why Is Client Correspondence Significant?
What Are the Well-known Ways Of Speaking With
Clients?

# Chapter 2
The following are 4 famous correspondence. channels
alongside their advantages.
Practice Proactive Client Correspondence.
Try not to Intrude on Your Clients
Have a Mindful Attitude.

# Chapter 3
**Convey the Manner in which Your Clients Need.**
Empower Questions.
Dispose of the Utilization of Negative Expressions.
How to prepare your client assistance group for better
correspondence?
Open Channels of Correspondence.
Be Aware of Your Crowd.

Be Straightforward answer Rapidly follow up. and be proactive .Use instructing devices to prepare representatives.

## Conclusion

# Introduction

Powerful correspondence lies at the core of durable client connections.
A solitary customized message is sufficiently strong to make clients your deep rooted fans. Then again, a postponed reaction can make them go to your business rivals.

With the ongoing blast in client care channels, organizations are battling to meet client assumptions. Furthermore, every brand on this planet is besieging existing as well as target clients with a huge number of promotions. Help work area programming is one of the most mind-blowing channels to eliminate mess and deal with your client assistance inquiries effectively from numerous channels.

Amid this tumult, a significant inquiry eclipses all others: How to discuss successfully with clients?
For powerful correspondence, you should know the intricate details of your items or administrations better than any other individual. Relational abilities like persistence, undivided attention, and a mindful mentality can likewise have a gigantic effect.
Indeed, that is not all!

Client assistance is an indispensable expertise for any business that needs to construct trust, devotion, and fulfillment among its clients. Nonetheless, it isn't sufficient to respond to questions or tackle issues.

You additionally need to discuss successfully with your clients, utilizing the right tone, style, and apparatuses. In this article, we will investigate a portion of the fundamental relational abilities for client support, and how you can apply them in your day-to-day collaborations.

# Chapter 1
## What Is Client Correspondence?

Client correspondence alludes to the interaction through which a business imparts significant data to its clients. Such corporations occur over well-known correspondence channels like email, telephone, live visits, virtual entertainment, online gatherings, client gateways, and numerous others.

Organizations speak with clients, mostly for two motivations to help them with their solicitations or grumblings and to advertise their new or corresponding items.

Presently you could ponder, why such countless organizations are chipping away at their client correspondence methodology.

The explanation is basic the shortfall of appropriate and convenient correspondence can rapidly heighten to fomented clients, diminished deals, and negative informal.

## What is Client Correspondence with The executives (CCM)?

Client Correspondence The board (CCM) alludes to a technique utilized by organizations to upgrade the nature of outbound interchanges.

The standards of CCM are rejuvenated with client-situated programming that stores all client correspondences in a focal spot. This guarantees that various divisions in an organization promoting, deals, money, and client support groups can intently screen all client communications.

CCM includes a system that integrates all your client-confronting workers. They can get to outbound discussions in a single spot and team up with different divisions to guarantee a smooth client experience.

## Why Is Client Correspondence Significant?

Today, how you speak with your clients can represent the moment of truth in your image. Further developed correspondence with clients can prompt blissful clients, rehash buys, and expand references.

As per a Microsoft study, around one of every three individuals says the main part of client support is talking with a learned and well-disposed specialist.

Nonetheless, factors like every minute of everyday accessibility, and the presence of numerous correspondence channels are similarly significant for client enchantment.

How about we rapidly see a few advantages of phenomenal client correspondence?
help clients continuously
advise them about significant updates
market your new items
enchant clients

**What Are the Well-known Ways Of Speaking With Clients?**

Current correspondence isn't restricted to customary channels, for example, composed letters or calls. Fast advancement has brought forth computerized channels like live visits, email, and web-based entertainment, and the sky is the limit from there.

Organizations speak with clients, mostly for two motivations to help them with their solicitations or grumblings and to advertise their new or corresponding items.

Presently you could ponder, why such countless organizations are chipping away at their client correspondence methodology.

The explanation is basic the shortfall of appropriate and convenient correspondence can rapidly heighten to fomented clients, diminished deals, and negative informal.

# Chapter 2

## The following are 4 famous correspondence channels alongside their advantages:

**Telephone**: The telephone is perfect for settling complex issues that can't be settled on different stations. For example, a specialized specialist can guide the client to make important investigating strides. Besides, nothing is more consoling than a quiet human voice.

**Email**: To get things into viewpoint, there are multiple billion email clients on the planet. Email is one of the most financially savvy correspondence channels accessible to humanity. Email strings can be utilized to follow the total client discussion.

**Live Talk**: Visit is one of the quickest strategies for speaking with clients. Client assistance reps can connect with clients continuously and investigate strategically pitching or upselling amazing open doors.

**Virtual Entertainment:** There is no question that the approaching ten years will be overwhelmed by web-based entertainment stages. There is a compelling reason to make any weighty venture as you just require a web-based entertainment page.

You can impart normal updates to clients and, surprisingly, run paid advancements to contact a more extensive crowd.

Instructions to Speak With Your Clients

Most business pioneers have a significant inquiry at the top of the priority list how ton o further develop correspondence with clients. While building a culture around powerful correspondence could take some time, it isn't generally so hard as you would naturally suspect.

Pass on Exact Data

For powerful correspondence and client support, passing on the right message or data is significant for any association.

Keep in mind, half-information can be risky for everybody. For example, if a client reaches you to ask about the means expected to work an electronic contraption, any mistaken data can end up being perilous.

It is the administration's liability to guarantee each staff part has something similar and the perfect proportion of data. They should pass on data about the time required to circle back so sensible client assumptions can be fixed all along.

It's not unexpected to see that giving similar data on each channel prompts a steady client experience. Any distinction might cost you a valuable client.

## Practice Proactive Client Correspondence

In many occurrences, clients are not happy with the help presented on the main endeavor. They could call you again to get their issues settled, and most likely once more.

In such cases, settling that issue could require some investment than the client's assumptions.

In such a situation where your client is hanging tight for your reaction, follow a proactive methodology.

The most ideal way to speak with clients is to keep them informed about each headway made.

By utilizing assist work area programming, you with canning share computerized warnings and cautions with clients as well as your inner representatives.

To energize proactive self-administration, you can make a committed information base. It incorporates pertinent assistance articles and FAQs for clients to determine their fundamental inquiries all alone.

## Try not to Intrude on Your Clients

At the point when clients are whining about an item or administration that has frustrated them, pay attention to them cautiously. Allow them to complete what they need to share and don't be in the middle between.

There is a decent chance that you could have heard a similar issue ordinarily and could know a fast answer for that. Notwithstanding, it is critical to recall that pointless Interferences can frustrate your clients, and cause them to feel less esteemed.

Possibly hinder when you experience any correspondence issues with clients. For example, you can obligingly request that

your clients stop if there is a language hindrance, specialized misfire, or their voice isn't discernible
Know pretty much everything there is to know about your item or administration
Clients will ask you absolutely everything, and you should be ready.

An absence of information about what you proposition can have an adverse consequence on the personalities of your clients. On the off chance that clients can detect that your workers don't comprehend your items or administrations alright, they could lose interest.

Guarantee your representatives go through ordinary instructional meetings and are knowledgeable about all items included as well as industry patterns.

Ask your item group to share fundamental data about new item dispatches so your forward-looking representatives can have something similar with clients.

**Have a Mindful Attitude**

While there are various ways of speaking with clients, for positive associations, you want to keep a mindful attitude.

While taking care of your clients, you can't simply stand to pass up vital subtleties as it can additionally exasperate what is going on.
Practice undivided attention and consistently focus on their words and inquiries.

Be mindful and on the off chance that you miss something, feel free to request that the client rehash the same thing.

During the cooperation cycle, guarantee you are available in a climate with the least interruptions. Shut out any pointless commotion and consistently keep a pen and paper helpful to make significant notes.

**Have a Mindful Attitude**

It might happen a couple of times that a client has posed you an inquiry and you do not know. Accordingly, you could neglect to furnish him with a proper response. Around then, it's smarter to sincerely concede that you need more data about this.

Promise the client that you will give him the fitting arrangement rapidly. On the off chance that is conceivable, inquire as to whether you can require them to be postponed to look for data from a higher rep or chief.

Try not to utilize words, for example, - "I think", "it very well may be", or "perhaps this one." Regular utilization of these words can make you sound confounded and less sure. Keep in mind, that any client would pick a fair reaction, regardless of whether it is negative, over a wrong untrustworthy reaction.

**Try not to Rush!**

It's not unexpected that by the day's end, you are worn out, and you could generally pursue faster routes while managing your clients. You could likewise feel free to trifle with their inquiries.

Notwithstanding, it is essential to recollect that although the individual may be your 100th client, you are the primary agent for them. Thus, be courteous and deal with them in the manner in which you took care of your most memorable client of the day.

We comprehend that each representative has a bunch of focuses to accomplish. Be that as it may, surging your method for finishing a call will make you look discourteous and amateurish. Plan your day ahead of time, take each cooperation in turn, and proposition your important opportunity to every client.

## Practice Tolerance

Being a client delegate, you ought to know why a client approaches you. They connect with you when they are uncertain and befuddled regarding your items or administrations.

Presently since your clients have put away their well-deserved cash, they could end up being furious because of any miscommunication or the inclination that they have been dealt with unreasonably.

During such occasions, the best anyone can hope for at this point is to rehearse one of the main client relational abilities persistence.

Toward the day's end, tolerance will assist you with tracking down the right arrangement and prevail upon your clients. Continuously recall that incredible assistance is superior to a fast one.

# Chapter 3

## Convey the Manner in which Your Clients Need

It is vital to take note of that clients are different in what they need and anticipate from a business. Why some could like to interface with a human specialist on the telephone, while others could use a chatbot to determine their fundamental issues.
Prior to managing their concerns, consistently ask them which language or mode they are alright with.

To make it significantly easier, you can pose inquiries like "What is the most effective way to be in contact with you?" or "Would you favor calling, messaging, or messaging?" Recollect, posing a basic inquiry can take you quite far.

Customize Each Collaboration
Personalization can be an integral asset to snatch client consideration and convey essential encounters.
As indicated by research, customized email crusades get 29% higher email open rates and 41% higher navigate rates contrasted with customary messages.

Welcome your clients by their most memorable name and offer substance in view of their preferences and interests.

Besides, even before your clients get in touch with you, ensure you have sufficient setting. Keep total client data from the items or administrations they have purchased from you to the historical backdrop of their past interchanges.

## Empower Questions

Correspondence is a two-way process that requires endeavors from the two finishes. To make any meeting more intuitive, urge clients to ask however many inquiries as they need.

All things considered, on the off chance that individuals are asking about your items or administrations, it's an extraordinary sign for your developing business.

You might respond to their inquiries at any point as well as get the valuable chance to instruct them about the different advantages and benefits.

Numerous clients don't see the worth in purchasing from a business except if they are taught about the profits.

Prior to finishing up a discussion, consistently inquire "Do you have any inquiries you might want to pose?" When client questions are responded to immediately, they can acquire genuinely necessary clearness on viewpoints, for example, item includes, accessible limits, conveyance plans, merchandise exchange, and that's just the beginning.

**Resolve Pressing Grumblings First**
Each organization, large or little, requirements to manage client grievances. There will be clients who commend you when something works perfectly and

reprimand you when they experience even a little issue.

Notwithstanding, the manner in which you handle pressing client protests can have a significant effect. Urge your representatives to determine objections according to the set Assistance Level Arrangements (SLA). Moreover, focus on client gives that request pressing goal.

## Dispose of the Utilization of Negative Expressions

At the point when you speak with a client, the whole standing of the business is in question and there ought to be a bad situation for cynicism.

Regardless of whether you experience an oppressive client, rehashing a similar could make you somewhat worse.

Each client who contacts your business needs to hear that there is an answer for their concerns. Utilizing words, for example, "we can't", "unrealistic" or "don't" will flag a failure to tackle an issue or an absence of mastery.

The steady utilization of negative words or expressions might additionally baffle clients and cause them to lose trust in your image.

Center around utilizing language that is positive and consoles your clients that they have come to the ideal locations.

Utilize Reliable Brand Jargon

For successful client care correspondence, you should utilize steady brand terms that clients can without much of a stretch handle.

The jargon used to speak with clients should match the vocab utilized on your business site, item lists, portable application, web-based entertainment pages, and so forth.

Involving unique or new terms for exactly the same things could befuddle clients and adversely influence their purchasing choices.

Train your staff to be predictable in the jargon they use across all correspondence channels.

Comprehend what you are fouling up

each business commits errors whether they are making the world's best item or essentially attempting to help a baffled client. In all actuality speaking with clients is difficult, particularly when they have better standards than any time in recent memory.

You will undoubtedly commit errors. Notwithstanding, it is essential to recognize such errors, gain from them, and try not to rehash them later on.

To all the more likely get it assuming clients are content with a connection, you can impart significant studies to them. This will offer them the chance to rate your administration and offer what they like or abhorrence in a flash.

Client input is an extraordinary method for understanding what you are fouling up and how clients might want to be conveyed.

Further develop Correspondence and Win Clients forever
Clients are the soul of any business and individuals who ought to make the biggest difference.

Hence, it turns into even more critical to effectively pay attention to what they need to say and keep them connected with for a wonderful communication.

Utilize the previously mentioned procedures and spills to speak with clients different correspondence channels.
Practice persistence, utilize a steady brand jargon, resolve critical issues, and in

particular work on your abilities through customary preparation.

Keep in mind, correspondence with an individual touch is the way to client achievement.

What would it be advisable for you to impart to the client about their issue? Clients ought to be offered the most proper arrangement as fast as could be expected.

Practice proactive correspondence and keep clients educated about the status of their issues ahead of time instead of hanging tight for them to reach you.

**How to prepare your client assistance group for better correspondence?**

It is vital to prepare your client support group on significant relational abilities like undivided attention, figuring out non-verbal prompts, regarding the feelings of clients, rehearsing persistence, sympathy, and so on.

How to further develop client relational abilities?
Here are a few ways to further develop your client's relational abilities:

Deal with each client like your first
Draw in with clients for a significant discussion
Train to work on your abilities
Take input to comprehend where you want to get to the next level
How does client correspondence fabricate reliability?

At the point when clients realize that they can without much of a stretch reach you whenever to enroll an issue or make a solicitation, they start to trust your business. This further outcomes in additional repurchases and references. In this way, you can assemble a multitude of faithful clients by proactively speaking with clients over channels they like.

Step-by-step instructions to Have More Viable Correspondence With Clients Everything organizations can improve in compelling correspondence with clients.

A 2022 report by Grammarly and The Harris Survey noticed that U.S. organizations are losing up to $1.2 trillion every year on account of unfortunate correspondence, both inside to their workers and partners as well as remotely to their clients and the market in general.

That is a gigantic misfortune being credited to a fixable issue with a straightforward cure: more successful correspondence.
Here, we'll think about the significance of correspondence with clients, the advantages of putting resources into better correspondence with your clients, and the kinds of data required while speaking with clients.

Why Powerful Client Correspondence Is Significant
Discussing actually with clients across all touchpoints, on the web and off, is imperative for any business. Clear and predictable correspondence brings about a

positive relationiship, and a superior client experience.

At last, it can likewise prompt more business for your organization through recurrent orders and even references to new clients.
Nonetheless, as per the 2022 Grammarly/Harris Survey report, 40% of information laborers and 17% of business pioneers say they're not certain while speaking with outside clients and sellers.

This absence of trust in correspondence with clients could be making organizations lose business, both new arrangements and existing clients. Furthermore, it comes down to the people who work in client assistance, promotion, and the contact place to ensure they take care of business while speaking with clients.

Powerful versus Insufficient Correspondence

How can you say whether your techniques for speaking with clients are functioning admirably? What's more, how might you let me know if your correspondence with clients is missing the mark? Recognizing proof of positive or unfortunate client correspondence with the executives is simple when you understand what signs to search for. Here are the absolute greatest hints:

Indications of Powerful Correspondence
High consumer loyalty appraisals (e.g., Consumer Loyalty Score (CSAT))
Solid client experience appraisals (e.g., Net Advertiser Score (NPS))
Positive remarks on client and audit locales

Fewer calls to client support
Vigorous recurrent business
Quality references to new clients
More profound client dependability

Expanded income
Indications of Insufficient Correspondence
Critical client agitate
More calls (and objections) to client
assistance
Expanded heightening of inbound calls to
supervisors
Negative audits via virtual entertainment,
survey destinations, and other
computerized channels
Low evaluations for client experience and
fulfillment (e.g., NPS, CSAT)
Declining or stale deals
Powerlessness to extend the client base

Step-by-step instructions to Have Better Correspondence With Clients
Luckily, there's a great deal you can do about further developing correspondence with your clients. One conventional strategy is to give delicate abilities to your association's client-confronting groups and client assistance staff, guaranteeing they're ready to take part in undivided attention and exhibit sympathy with your clients when required.

Regardless of whether your organization is as of now successful at correspondence, there is generally an open door to up your group's down.

Numerous answers for lifting the nature of client correspondence today include innovation. For example, via robotizing certain parts of client assistance utilizing apparatuses like computerized reasoning (man-made intelligence)- controlled chatbots, your clients can interface with the data and assist them with requiring all the more rapidly.

Furthermore, if the help they require includes chatting with a human, the computerization of routine undertakings will give your representatives the additional opportunity to dedicate to conveying customized administration.

**Open Channels of Correspondence**
In this advanced time, there have never been more ways for your business to speak with clients.

Email or instant messages, visit capabilities on your site, online showcase and paid promotions, and web-based entertainment channels are only a few choices.

Furthermore, remember the telephone: Exploration shows that 60% of clients settle on a telephone decision to a business while considering high-stakes buys, similar to protection and cars. Much of the time, your call community tasks will furnish your clients with their initial feeling of your business, so it's beneficial to make ventures, remembering for innovation, to assist with guaranteeing that the experience is a heavenly one.

Imaginative innovation is working in many call communities today, assisting businesses to convey more compelling correspondence with clients. Invoca's simulated intelligence-fueled

Call following and examination stage, for instance, gives clear and succinct accessible records of calls that organizations can use to affirm they're successfully conveying the perfect messages to their clients at the ideal time.

These experiences additionally can be utilized for continuous call community staff preparing, and for changing contents to further develop specialist execution later on.

**Be Aware of Your Crowd**

Clients are frequently inclined toward brands they feel a unique interaction with. If they have an involvement in a brand or delegates leave them needing or are out and out poor, it could harm the client-brand relationship before it even gets an opportunity to bloom.

Ensure any colleagues liable for connecting straightforwardly with your clients comprehend the significance of conveying customized correspondence to them and exceeding everyone's expectations to cause them to feel esteemed. Likewise, put resources into the proper preparation and devices that will assist them with giving positive client encounters.

Tune in and Pose Explaining Inquiries

Try not to simply pay attention to clients. Participate in undivided attention. That includes concentrating on what a client is talking about and holding on until they're done to come to a meaningful conclusion or pose an inquiry.

Undivided attention requires focusing on what the speaker is talking about. It is additionally significant: Explaining what the client has said eliminates any uncertainty, and will assist you with abstaining from with nothing to do in settling an issue agreeable to them to Get clarification on some pressing issues.

## Be Straightforward

Great correspondence originates from telling the truth and is straightforward. If you can't tackle a client's concern, be forthright about it. Show compassion, and tell the client you will give your best to assist them with associating with the suitable individual or group who might have the option to help them.

Clients perceive that a few issues might require a more extended fix, incorporating different collaborations with help staff. They will be more quiet with this cycle assuming you're straightforward with them all along.

**Answer Rapidly**

Try not to stand by too long to even think about answering client correspondence! Besides the fact that your clients merit a quick reaction, most will likewise anticipate it.

A basic guideline of thumb in business today is that messages ought to get a reaction in 24 hours or less. Answering quicker is better, obviously. Regardless of whether you have a response, let the client in on what you're figuring out about their problem. Likewise, consider utilizing a robotized answer to recognize that a client's email has been gotten, particularly assuming that it shows up beyond your client care collaboration hours. Provide the client with some signs of when they could get a reaction.

**Follow Up and Be Proactive**

The last impression the client gets in any client correspondence is pretty much as significant as the first. You might be enticed to feel that since you've settled the issue, is it finished, and you've conveyed a good client experience. Yet, consistently make that additional stride. Proactively inquiring as to whether they have different issues requiring consideration or just saying thanks to them for their call can go far toward improving client care. (Also, remember to inquire as to whether they'd give input on their experience, for example, through an email overview.)

Put forth Quantifiable Objectives and Screen Them Routinely

An unquestionable requirement for successful client correspondence the executives is being able to quantify accomplishment. Settle the measurements that can influence your client correspondence the most and set up a framework to routinely quantify those measurements.

Key measurements for a call place activity, for example, could incorporate the consequences of short, post-call client overviews, return call information demonstrating the number of clients that expected to get back to until their concern was settled, and the number of calls that must be raised.

Mechanize Quality Affirmation to All the more likely Survey Specialists Execution

There are not many fresh opportunities to get things right in client care.

That is the reason precisely measuring your representatives' exhibition and utilizing that information to further develop the client experience is so fundamental. Client care groups can utilize computer-based intelligence to drive improved results by scoring 100 percent of calls, rather than simply a little example.

Computer-based intelligence can likewise assist with lessening case volume by dissecting terms inside call records to distinguish issues at scale.

Test Invoca specialist scorecard created by artificial intelligence

Likewise, you need your contact community staff to be prepared to assist with directing clients toward a change if they're looking for data to assist them with making a buy.

In a new Invoca review, 87% of purchasers expressed conversing with an individual on the telephone to respond to questions caused them to feel more sure about making costly or thought-about buys, as opposed to purchasing straightforwardly on the web. To measure call-taking care of value and increment transformations, numerous organizations are presently utilizing simulated intelligence-fueled discussion knowledge programming to acquire an understanding into each contact place association.

## Use Instructing Devices to Prepare Representatives

Training your staff is basic to receive the rewards of good correspondence with clients and boost your group's exhibition, particularly in a call community climate. What's more, you can utilize information assembled through man-made intelligence to make instructing apparatuses for your call community staff.

For instance, Invoca's simulated intelliintelligence-controlledsion knowledge stage assists call with focusing specialists and their administrators cooperate all the more successfully to recognize and stop persistent vices from the beginning and assemble great ones.

Specialists can audit the records and accounts from their discussions with clients, which Invoca naturally gives following each call. They likewise get moment admittance to simulated intelliintelligence-producedcores, which improves self-instructing.

Invoca permits you to give your deals specialists continuous remarks on their presentation

Specialists can undoubtedly impart records and accounts to their directors to demand their feedback and direction.

Remote training is likewise a breeze with Invoca in it can access and remark straightforwardly on accounts and records in the stage.

They can give criticism on unambiguous minutes and use email warnings to label specialists.

Make Brand Jargon and Item/Administration Books of scriptures

A brand or item/administration book of scriptures lays out a bunch of rules representatives are supposed to keep while speaking with clients about a brand, item, or administration.

These rules can assist your groups with passing on clear and predictable messages while communicating with your clients.

A common brand book of scriptures contains an abundance of brand-related data including designs, logo medicines, and letterhead layouts — however, the genuine incentive for client-confronting representatives is the information it contains.

Finish Discussions With Clear Subsequent stages

Try not to leave clients in an in-between state. Ensure you impart what steps you, or the guest, should take closely to determine an issue. If a goal to the issue will require a couple of days to process or another person should contact the client, make sense of that.

If the client has a reasonable image of the subsequent stages, it's doubtful they'll have to get back to it.

# Conclusion

Practice Compassion and Tolerance

The delicate abilities that client assistance groups and others need most to convey praiseworthy client correspondence are persistence and compassion.

Clients esteem organizations that are genuinely mindful and try to grasp their issues and make arrangements. Feelings are significantly more significant in the period of simulated intelligence, and artificial intelligence can assist you with affirming your representatives are giving them all to ensure clients feel great, esteemed, and heard.

For instance, Invoca's discussion knowledge arrangement permits organizations to set up looks for key expressions in telephone discussions. To be certain your representatives are utilizing compassionate expressions like "I get it" or "Thank you for your understanding," Invoca's Sign Revelation component can help.

www.ingramcontent.com/pod-product-compliance
Lightning Source LLC
Chambersburg PA
CBHW050517290526
45786CB00007B/2597